Hello World!

Greetings in 42 Languages Around the Globe!

by Manya Stojic

Cartwheel
B·O·O·K·S®

SCHOLASTIC INC.

New York   Toronto   London   Auckland   Sydney
Mexico City   New Delhi   Hong Kong   Buenos Aires

This book is dedicated to Amineta from Togo and all other children like her who have experienced slavery.
— M.S.

Illustrations for this book were produced in Acrylics.

Copyright © 2002 by Manya Stojic.
All rights reserved. Published by Scholastic Inc.
Created and produced by Boxer Books Ltd. & Tribal Design.
SCHOLASTIC, CARTWHEEL BOOKS, and associated logos are trademarks and/or
registered trademarks of Scholastic Inc.

Library of Congress Cataloging-in-Publication Data available

ISBN 0-439-36202-4

10 9 8 7 6 5 4 3 2 1   02 03 04 05 06

Printed in Singapore
First printing, November 2002

How to Use this Book:

It is simple to learn to say "hello" in many different languages.

The languages featured in this book span the world from west to east—across the continents from the Americas to Australia.

The greetings can be pronounced by using the phonetic spellings beneath each translation. For example, the French word for "hello" is "bonjour," which is pronounced {bohn-ZHOOR}. If you meet people who speak French, don't be shy—they will love to hear you greet them in their own language.

Enjoy saying "hello" in all the languages with your friends and family!

"Hello"

is a very magical word.
Everyone says "hello."
I hope you will try to
say it in as many
languages as you can.
Pass on the magic
and make people smile!

Aloha!
{a-LOH-hah}

Hawaiian

Kiana!
{kee-AH-nah}   **Inuktitut**

O-si-yo!

{oh-see-YOH}

Cherokee

Hello!

{he-LOH}

English

Olaj!

{OH-lah}

Yucateco

Oy!

{oy-EE}

Guajajára

Hylo!
{he-LOH}

Welsh

Olá!

{oh-LAH}

Portuguese

¡Hola!

Spanish

{OH-lah}

Bonjour!

{bohn-ZHOOR}

Hallo!
{he-LOH}

Danish
Hei!
{HAY}

Finnish
Hei!
{HAY}

Hei!
{HAY}
Norwegian

Hej!
{HAY}
Swedish

Guten Tag!

{GOO-ten TAHG}

{CHOW}

Zdravo!

{ZDRAH-voh}

Geia Sou!
{YAH soo}

Greek

Zdravstvuite!

Russian {ZZDRAHST-vet-yah}

Merhaba!
{MER-hah-bah} Turkish

Shalom!

Hebrew

{shah-LOHM}

Salaam

{sah-LAHM}

Selam!

{se-LAHM}

Bafia
Wayumbe!
{wah-YOOM-beh}

Bambara
I ni bara!
{ee nee BAH-rah}

Ci yi bak!
{see yee BAHK}

Dinka

Sawubona!
{sah-woo-BOH-nah}

Zulu

27

Kayira be!

Mandinka {kah-HEE-rah beh}

Jambo!
{JAM-boh}

Swahili

Bengali
Nomoskaar!
{NOH-moh-skahr}

Hindi
Namasté!
{nah-mah-STAY}

Tamil
Vanakkam!
{vah-nah-KUM}

Urdu
Adaab!
{ah-DAHB}

Sawatdi!
{sah-waht-DEE} Thai

Chào!

{DZHOW}

Vietnamese

Níh hâo!
{nee HAOW}   **Mandarin**

Konnichiwa!

Japanese   {koh-NEE-chee-wah}

Annyoung Hasimnikka!

{an-YOH HAS-him-ni-kah}

Dada Namona!

{dah-dah nah-MOH-nah}

Arru!

{ah-ROO}

Arabana

Kia Ora!

Maori

{KEE-ah OH-rah}

INDEX

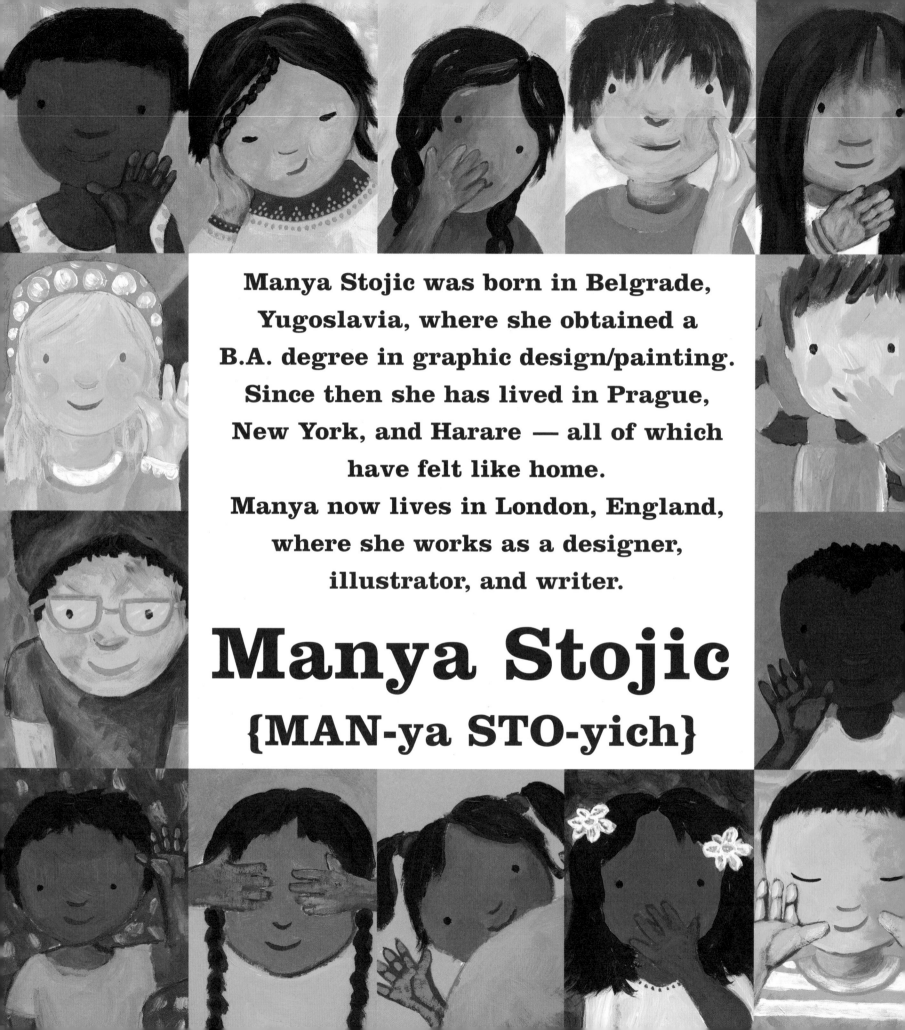

Manya Stojic was born in Belgrade, Yugoslavia, where she obtained a B.A. degree in graphic design/painting. Since then she has lived in Prague, New York, and Harare — all of which have felt like home.

Manya now lives in London, England, where she works as a designer, illustrator, and writer.

Manya Stojic
{MAN-ya STO-yich}